SHIMA

SHIMA

POEMS

SHŌ YAMAGUSHIKU

McClelland & Stewart

McClelland & Stewart and colophon are registered trademarks of Penguin Random House Canada Limited.

Published simultaneously in the United States of America.

Library and Archives Canada Cataloguing in Publication data is available upon request.

ISBN: 978-0-7710-1092-7
ebook ISBN: 978-0-7710-1488-8

Cover design by Dylan Browne
Cover images: Rob Sato
Typeset in Agmena by Sean Tai
Printed in Canada

The definition on page ix is excerpted from *Okinawan-English Wordbook: A Short Lexicon of the Okinawan Language with English Definitions and Japanese Cognates* by Mitsugu Sakihara et al. (University of Hawai'i Press, 2006). The quoted material on page xi is excerpted from *Paris, When It's Naked* by Etel Adnan (The Post-Apollo Press, 1993). The quoted material on page 5 is excerpted from "Two Poems" by Takara Ben, translated by Katsunori Yamazato and Frank Stewart in *Living Spirit: Literature and Resurgence in Okinawa* (University of Hawai'i Press, 2011). The quoted material on page 17 is excerpted from *We Must Learn to Sit Down Together and Talk About a Little Culture: Decolonising Essays, 1967-1984* © Sylvia Wynter, reproduced by permission of Peepal Tree Press. The quoted material on page 33 is from Sakiyama Tami, translated by Huei-chu Chu in Chu's article "Deauthenticating Indigeneity" (*Amerasia Journal*, vol. 41, no. 1, 2015, pp. 37–52). The quoted material on page 40 is from an unknown author, translated by Taira Bintaro in *My Favorite Okinawan Poems* (1969).

McClelland & Stewart,
a division of Penguin Random House Canada Limited,
a Penguin Random House Company
www.penguinrandomhouse.ca

1 2 3 4 5   28 27 26 25 24

Penguin
Random House
McCLELLAND & STEWART

for 杉夫 and 清臣

CONTENTS

shima, n: 1. A village; a community.
2. One's home village. 3. One's fief.
4. An island.

An ancestral forest within me stirs my
memory and makes life untenable.

— ETEL ADNAN

SHIMA

My father stands in his yard holding my hair. Down the sloping crescent, a tangle of strands fastens me to a rainbow. The border dissolves at my feet, feet break, and we disappear. I am far away now, blistering. My father is still holding. Each month away from that ledge gathers in my scalp, drying into dust.

Every evening my father plucks my hair. A cloud of disturbed thoughts darkens the sky, bats flying from the recesses. With the hair on my scalp my father finds a rhythm. A love so stretched, without a limit, I feel as though I might bleed.

Between each note, we swim a grotto of melancholy. My father is in a remembering trance. I am a continent away. My hair is impossibly long. I think I am free. So high like this. I believe I am untethered. My mind is enclosed, proud and square. My thoughts, a line of trees stripped of their bark.

I stand atop a pile of discarded lumber. I can see the tracks of wooden friends, strangers, I can see you. Here, a desiccated river road. And here, naked trees and everywhere else, too.

My father keeps plucking the notes. The notes gather into a wave. The desiccated road and the current of my father's clutch play, one and the same.

I walk until one morning I stop, fall and begin again like water. Something is promised to me. An osprey plummets into the ocean and my father begins to sing.

amerika-yuu

Today through a breach in the encircling reef
the son who departs dreaming
of joining a revolution in a northern city
someday will return on the tide —
the son who renounced a village
that still believes in the spirit world
and the gods. In the same village,
the mother never gives up waiting.

— Takara Ben
(translated by Katsunori Yamazato and Frank Stewart)

In the americas, the chaplain of science divides rhythm into equal parts

In the interstices, ancestors plummet to their deaths

A scholar says a house of diasporic okinawans is an impossible condition

My family's house is made up of cement minutes and silent hours

At the end of his rope, a rogue cousin slips drunkenly into the night

He is now a new sound in the ground, oddly breaking the chaplain's rhythm

Beside a hydrangea bush, the cousin stretches into a metal sleep

A net spread serendipitous with refusal, he catches a plummeting ancestor

a vastness

disappears

abandons me

to a cloudless night

all the stars

turn sleep's path

away from me

in the distance, nikkei boys

loosen laughter

an island blowing

hot and brassy

from my

tongue

Departure hoists its tattered flag.

I vacate the subject of my sentences. I abandon my seat of potential. A scattering of eyes, the sticky floor of the commuter rail. With my own blood I paint a picture of a disenchanted revolutionary on the train's dirty windows. A reactionary stares back at me obscuring _____ & _____ leaks along the seats of the train.

I believe the world. I want you to believe that I am breaking from the world.

Again, *can't you see, my hands are no longer bloody.*

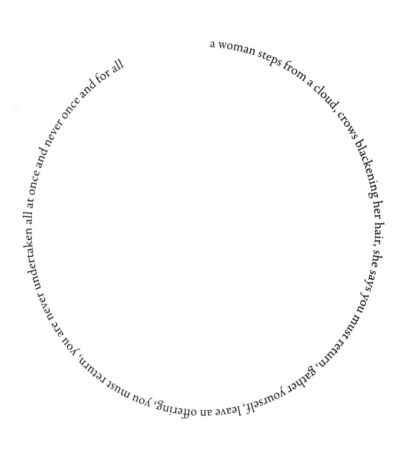

a woman steps from a cloud, crows blackening her hair, she says you must return, gather yourself, leave an offering, you must return, you are never undertaken all at once and never once and for all

the priestess and yagachi gather in a clearing

a small prophecy bursting

from their forested navels

the boy will return!

the boy will return!

the public peers into the clearing

murmuring

the boy will return!

the boy will return!

the priestess and yagachi roast yams on an open fire

preparing for night's curtain to fall

An overcast morning, a pair of budding trees elongates in me.

Their branches slide a tomb through my grandmother's hollowed chest.

The lining of my father's stomach turns to bark.

My great-grandfather says, *you will never take the trees from me!*

The central government spears timber to my father's timber heart.

The trees slip from the forest's grasp.

A man scatters three grains of rice on my grave's future plot.

He leaves the next morning clutching a fine line.

He hoists himself across the ocean.

Behind him, the forest roars in disappearance.

yamatu-yuu

The majority of us (writers in exile) keep on talking [. . .] and when our people at home read what we have written about them, they cannot recognize themselves any more.

— C.L.R. James
(cited by Sylvia Wynter)

I grasp the lone scraggly hibiscus bush. A man slips inside my body and falls into a single grain of sand. I am looking down at my grassy self in his watering eyes. Above us one bloom opens red to the plateau's sky. My only flag, a sputtering waterfall, rises un-prospected waving and weighing on me. The man and I wear shame softly and for a moment it emulsifies. I begin to sweat. The man licks my shoulder clean. The sun has reached its apex and I am stiff, difficult as ever, pointing crooked west. I am a compass pulling across the inland sea, over the desert to the smiling city by the coast, greeting the gaping ocean, trawling, sifting for that rock of an island, as if through a searching explosion, it might be mine

I know my auntie is tired

but I ask one more favour

she calls forth the spirits

carving their transitions

into the whacked pulsing

of failing ventricles

our excesses splattered

across her canvas where

the fallen paint portraits

her heart hangs with

pastel sadness — still

she compasses us

back to love

past the second hill, ten paces to the left

of the walnut tree the ones we know

constellate there, you'll find a

stone set to keep spirit from

wandering, say

the flowers lay

a prayer

yet, upon arrival we are not

met with closure but a breaking

brilliant of light shooting skywards

boasting a shimmering coat

of a million competing colours

Uncle,

Forgive me for shining this light
into your graveyard of an eye

Where are you?
I am looking to return

There is a dugong drowning in the desert
a mushroom cloud gathering dust in your closet

This placid lake keeps leaking
sepia ink and smoke

flares, ammunition shells
cover the rainforested floor

You are being vaulted into currency
carved of timber bones, this relic

that you will become, you thought

you had a choice

I scanned your data

it became a straight-jacket into a Place

the records are my privatized playground

I hold you there, running, thinning like hair

back and forth negotiating these words

      as ancestors

            as pixels

                  as things without morals

But after all, it is 2023.

      Shouldn't you be in your grave?

Message to The Root Ancestor or Things We Call Silence :

_____ never spoke about _____

(his daughter)   (masako)

_____ ridiculed _____

_____ lived only with sadness   (taro)

                    (kintaro)

(violence)

          (haruko)   (war)

_____ stole _____

(her language)

_____ flattened _____

                                        (his body)

(sumiko)

                              (tomiko)

_____ violated _____

                    _____ found pleasure in _____

                              (uto)

me and my brother

we circle the lone tree by the fountain

we do not dare touch, yet we admire

our isolation
our collective
our impossible

No Loitering, squad cars everywhere

towards gentleness
we, legislation

speaking of a misplaced lighter, a failed manifesto

no innocence in the sun
no criminal in the tide

beneath our feet the dry red earth forms

a hand reaching through

the earthquake's remnants

clutching a shattered lapis lazuli

I learn to fashion my mouth as

    a market of transactions

I learn my endless argument

    with the ocean is impossible

I divine no sweet potato

    I drink no time

I offer myself in sewers

    and streetcars

I wander down Crenshaw

    looking to buy an ancestor

My father holds my hair, the evening's last ray of sunshine falls into a furious fight. I am disintegrating down the coast, my scalp ablaze. With song, with waves, I break shoeless off Santa Monica Pier. Barnacles knife, starfish grenade: their sentience sharp inside of me as the ocean floor deepens. The lights of a container ship flash across the rolling current. Above deck humans shudder, their stilted grammar pulling against the moon. A current of fairies casts a lunar net, blessing a trench of bioluminescence. All opens between sea and sky. Storm petrels deposit me into the shape of a lone tropicbird. I see my great-grandmother, her white wings. We make a union so precise, a flood of heaving chests is all that we have ever known. I search for a shard of gentleness, anglerfish brandishing themselves against my thighs. I stumble into the carcass of the *Kieta Maru*, the bones of the silvery dead rattling. I mistake the ship's barnacle-encrusted anchor for a lost treasure. Lusting over steel's certainty, I shove the rusted prongs inside of me. The crown of humans forming the ocean floor shifts and now the ship is careening, disappearing down the Mariana Trench. A rancid cave in me, all that remains as blood pours. A cadre of neon jellyfish. I am tickled numb by tentacles; I am hilarious with pain. A darkness birthing another darkness inside the forts of my childhood becoming oceanic or becoming womb.

uchinaa-yuu

Isn't it that I have been hesitating about going to O Island because I unconsciously believe that the island is myself? [. . .] It is because I have sensed my true self within the heartrending sorrow and vexation, and felt my grandmother's gloomy gaze.

— Sakiyama Tami
(translated by Huei-chu Chu)

by pounding cane

my people

step in time, parading eagerly

amidst nostalgia's

ghostly flags

everywhere indigenous regalia sprouts

from concrete chests

Naha City opening my brutalist heart

as we journey

through limestone

we fortress *our royal womb*

this place that precedes all,

and for a moment I fade

from my body

made weak,

too taken to notice a celestially

ordained scribe is engraving the parameters

of home in the blanking

reaches

of my cerebellum

I am fixated inside a sun-soaked vision

and in the city below, a restless man

is beating his wife

every time the words

peaceful and *kingdom*

collide

amidst my solar delusion

a faceless man passes

through the castle gates,

rising above the parade

he sheds his plastic suit

and dons a brass coloured robe

the robe, commissioned

by the island's

cheering thousands . . .

the faceless man has his

hand on my shoulder

(he has his hand on

everyone's shoulder)

the faceless man has his

hand on my thigh

(he has his hand on

everyone's thigh)

the faceless man whispers:

be still

I will clothe you in my fibres, let us exalt in your traditional name.

but everything pulsates

and in the harbour in me

blood roils

a shuddering
prefecture
bearing
down

If you want to dye me at all,
Dye me as dark as crow's feather.
If you want to dye me but light,
Pray don't touch me at all.

— author unknown
(translated by Taira Bintaro)

groping a shadowy hamlet

by the small of the sea

skirting boulders

tiptoeing bones

bound for the grave

passing estuarine fields

(chrysanthemum

or sugarcane

I don't care)

the night's pinnacle

its concern:

a soldier,

ready for harvest

a soldier's load:

a fluorescent light

a hideous tower

and the dead wearing our skin

drumming the night's hide

from the cradle, the boy and I are enlisted

to sentinel male power

we stand on bulging lineages

eldest sons narrowing into the island's wide night

living inside a mirage of departure

genealogies branded

across stomachs bursting with inertia

we are meant to cluster trees into families of worth

we are meant to name fallen branches:

detritus, deviant, difficult

that which is made

to pulverize

to pulp

the boy and I sit in Urasoe Park

our thoughts punctuated   the roar of fighter jets overhead

the sound first obscene then frightfully

normal

the jets bound for

U.S. Marine Corps
Air Station Futenma

swallow benevolent dreams and spit them out across asia

arrows rain down

on Vietnam

and Korea

(then, of course, but again, when?)

the metal din overhead seems to say:

it is alright, go ahead now, forget who you are

our conversation

deflates, shallows

living inside occupation's labyrinth,

the boy and I have searched

frantic for exits

cliffs high enough

drinks strong enough

knives sharp enough

lusting for *elsewhere*

hostage to the idea of an ocean free of water

a mother chases her child across the park

the boy in front of me speaks in omissions:

a northern cape

a ruinous site

an illegitimate child

I dream of the boy

walking off the cliff emboldened

by a storm

but gravity refuses his body

and a tangle of ropes and roots

sprouts from Cape Hedo's

rock-encrusted scalp

fastening him to life

he is held in the

brutality of nirai kinai's

perfection, suspended forever

for all the faithful to see

At dinner, my father tells my mother *melancholy*. For the first time he appears to be looking at his melancholy from outside of his melancholy as though he never realized it was lodged there. He decides on something more. He sculpts it into a song.

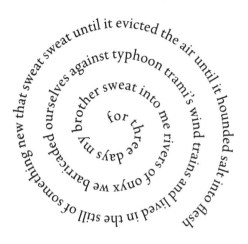

for three days my brother sweat into me rivers of onyx and lived in the still of something new that sweat sweat until it evicted the air until it hounded salt into flesh and we barricaded ourselves against typhoon trami's wind trains and

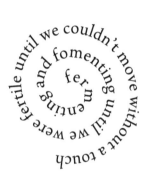

fermenting and fomenting until we were fertile until we couldn't move without a touch

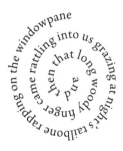

and then that long woody finger came rattling into us grazing at night's tailbone came rapping on the windowpane

We dig bloody moons from the horizon

Prayers erupting from our skin.

We climb these tall shoots and stems

Back-bend down to green ground.

I can tell my brother is light and heat

I forget mirrors and my hatred of trees.

I tell my brother, the earth does

And does not need saving.

And down by the water

Songbirds in the shrubs

And kingfisher tumbling

And twisting, falling

Free from tree to tree.

yanbaru-yuu

My hair calcifies, watery flesh floods my lungs. Coral claims me. I am molten, an ocean marking final decisions. The tides wear away at my yearning. I no longer need the violence of spectacle. I find comfort in the fractal return, this underwater constellation. The sharp staff of addiction begins to fade. I breathe in hues of sage. I wrap myself in the blue of this day. With the caress of a thousand fishes, I learn the fleeting nature of love. I build a reef around my body. I forget the names of political parties and public holidays. From time to time, people peer down at me through glass-bottomed boats. In their shadow, I see flashes of wicked things. I remember how they live their lives by building walls. How far can a house of bricks be from shame, how far from guilt, how far from revenge.

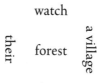

watch
enclose words an eager
poet

watch
enclose lands an eager
politician

watch
their forest a village
lose

a dugong's ghost rides a moaning

violet current, a surf curls

into my father's song

the divided wind

runs laden with

cries of coral

cleaved, uprooted, smothered

I see the elders holding an empire on their backs

aren't you tired? I ask

as if collapse is ever an option

as if a placid sea holds any indication of our latent fury

the ocean floor is soft as mayonnaise yet

an atomic mandate demands that

this bay must bear a commander's thousand loads

a concrete platform

to launch a blanket

of white memory across

the asian continent

no place for wayward sadness

only a devouring

radiated genocide

to name a friend

is to prepare for

their eventual departure,

to attempt to love

this disappearing sea

another impending goodbye

to know a friend entirely

is to attempt to

swallow the ocean

to know an entire people is to have

no choice except to drown,

so I make a tenuous life

of peace knowing

creation is simply

another

word for

failure

Once a year the villagers gather at the water's edge, the women knee-deep and full of prayer, the men flying across the bay. Heeding their invocation, the sea god arrives riding high the stirrups of a dugong. The pair, god and dugong, come veiled in schools of fish. The fish jump into the villagers' nets glinting with sun, the shimmers of the season approaching.

Some years, the pair, god and dugong, arrives sombre and alone.

I return to the place the door

once was
                              cobbling together

        my makeshift ceremony

July 10, 1877 — Taro Yamashiro
(山城) is born in the village of
Tanna on the shores of Sa-a Bay.

July 6, 1904 — Taro leaves Tanna
on a boat bound for Mexico via
New Caledonia. He works the
coal mines as a contract labourer
for La Compañia Japonesa Mexi-
cana de Comercio y Colonización
in Coahuila, Mexico. Taro flees
from the mine's exploitative
labour conditions with a group
of Okinawan workers across the
border into the United States.
His daughter's son fathers me.

February 28, 1971 — Taro dies
in Los Angeles, never having
returned to the island where he
was born.

A recurring dream:
from a collective ghost,
an emerging self
from a blowing storm,
an advancing line,
from a depraved descendant,
a desperate pounding

March 6, 1900 — Uto Yamashiro (山城) is born in the village of Tanna on the shores of Sa-a Bay. Sometime around 1919, Uto joins her husband in the United States, eventually settling with her family in California's Imperial Valley. When war breaks out, Uto's family are uprooted and sent to live as prisoners at Poston War Relocation Center on land within the boundaries of the Colorado River Indian Reservation. Uto's daughter's son fathers me.

Uto returns to her home village once in her life. She makes the journey alone.

April 30, 1971 — Uto passes away in Los Angeles, roughly two months after her husband.

With limited vision, Uto might appear to follow behind her husband through the archive. Yet, her life exceeds the hard scaffolding that often marks a man's existence. She does not need the materiality of data to become legible in the realm of the ancestors.

A recurring dream:
a forest dense with laughter
a clearing full of presence

I greet my uncle at the harvest festival.

He turns his back.

The village spreads itself for

the feverish water dream.

The forest blossoms with my failures.

I am ravenous

for a golden tradition. I am brimming

with fangs and mandates.

My eyes are cameras. My feet are

clubs. The village

is suspended above the water. I am

stroking its underbelly.

I am stealing glances at my

own grave.

I am forcing my body inside a

closed ritual. I am

prying at everything that resembles

a hinge or a door. I am

squeezing a child's throat, demanding

to know why my language

has no name.

I am breaking over an elder's

     head. I am

waking in a living room

     my hands roving

past the family altar.

     I am glimpsing the emperor's

smile in a villager's tired face.

     I am swallowing

whole offerings of fruit

     meant for the gods.

I am picking flesh from my teeth.

     The village is tilting

on its axis. It is turning.

     All its organs are

spilling across the bay.

     I am taking the sharpest stick

and poking the root

     ancestor. I am

insisting that if he awakens

     I will have something

useful to say.

I count the revolving vertebrae covering the hills and slide my hands up and down my tortured spine. I wade through liquid debts and crimson greens. The trees form a sprawling rosary, each branch a shivering bead. I mark the forest's death and devastation, caressing where the exiled ones once lived, their lives speculated as lumber and carted away to build majestic trade ships and towering southern castles.

Over the years I have learned to contort my body flat against the forest's heaving chest. The trees taught me intimacy when the waking world ran from me. Now, roots have sprouted like hair from my head and they have become roads. This forest is every forest

and wide roots can show me love

I enter where the gully yawns its fragile windpipe to the bottomless world. The oldest living one has told the most recently dead one that I am coming. The most recently dead one has told the one who died before them that I am coming. This message travels until my people have abandoned their names

the cliffs above are steep with grievances as I lay down an offering, as I concede:

this whimpering ocean

might hold my ashen body

underneath falling shadows

this resplendent rain

a solid moon

incants a lockless safe

graciously holding

my leaking life

the surf sweeps the hollows of my back

I see the moon and a shard of me in all their faces

fishing towards the war

Who is that close!

Who is that far!

I plead for a translator's witness

Please wrap this lament in satin!

Please keep these intestines concealed!

after spirit after spirit after spirit after

the boy who never speaks grasps my hand

with his dawn, I have a slivering chance

to be reborn as sick fish with strange fins

we might-have-been ancestors

jump against the moonlight

circling the brackish bay

a school travelling

through a watery shrine

queer and

barren of offerings

evading my place in the confines of lineage

I glimpse a grave,

all this could have schooled me

A boy appears in my father's yard. My father is sitting drinking a beer. The boy presents a tattered case from which my father plucks a worn three-stringed instrument. The boy sits in front of my father and listens intently to his voice dance across a lilting rhythm. The boy's eyes wide as sun turns to moon. Finally, my father releases my hair.

ACKNOWLEDGEMENTS

My gratitude to:

the forest for the incessant whispers and the ocean for the relentless rides

山城 relations in Okinawa, Yokohama, Los Angeles, São Paulo, and anywhere else they might be, whose cosmic ancestral tissue forms the bodies of these poems

my editor Canisia Lubrin for shining a light so brilliant and precise into me that it couldn't help but to illuminate the shape of these poems, even when I repeatedly tried to flee from them

Kaie Kellough for watering belief into these poems when they were seeds, not yet broken free from the ground

Brandon Shimoda for the generous and expansive questions that led me outside of a world that kept closing in around me

Cecily Nicholson for modeling for me the careful ethics of a beating heart

Jane Shi for returning with me again and again to the questions of poetic craft + politics

Punam Khosla for insisting that beauty remain with me at a time I desired for it to be destroyed

Joseph Kamiya for persevering with me through the most difficult parts of our shared diasporic memory

Lee Maracle for reawakening within me the importance of story

M. Jacqui Alexander for infusing my writing dreams with fibres of freedom

Victor (who appears as *my brother* in several poems) for the protective incantations

Kelly Joseph, Rebecca Rocillo, and the entire team at M&S for their patience and expertise and for always going above and beyond to uplift the words in this collection

my parents for my most difficult and beautiful inheritance

my sister for being my guardian through these seasonal typhoons

Cato St. Malo for embodying the place where the ocean meets the water, the place that never fails to bring me back to life

Rob Sato, whose artwork graces the cover of this collection

Patrick, Tasha, Kayla, Katie, and Bri for protecting me at my most vulnerable

Letitia, Emma, David, and Baraka for always ensuring the vibration is correct

Uncle Mike, Aunt Jill, Aunt Sandy, Aunt Eileen, Aunt Rain, Uncle Ali, Auntie Alice, Auntie Mary, Oma, Paulette, Rhonda, Lynne, James, Jen, Maki, Mutsuki, Cindy, Yukimasa, Sayuri, Bean, Reyna, Sam, Ruben, Shigeru, Yoshi, Riku, Kazu, Ravyn, and Izumi for offering me a place to rest on this long journey

Yuko Yamauchi, Nicole Yakashiro, Wesley Ueunten, Kenji Tokawa, Kai Cheng Thom, Darcy Tamayose, ŚW̱,XELOSELWET, Shaunga Tagore, Audra Simpson, Christina Sharpe, Alana Sayers, January Rogers, PEPAḴIYE, Chiedza Pasipanodya, Joshua Ngenda, Nozomi Nakaganeku Saito, Cindy Mochizuki, Sean Miura, Angela May, Wendy Matsumura, K'eguro Macharia, David Lewis-Peart, Grayson Lee, Shabina Lafleur-Gangji, Gnanushan Krishnapillai, Ben Kobashigawa, Rosina Kazi, Debby Kajiyama, Inoue Mayumo, Daniel Iwama, Erica Isomura, Lisa Hofmann-Kuroda, Augusto Higa Oshiro, Essex Hemphill, Hiromi Goto, Neema Githere, Ayano Ginoza, Tomoki Fukui, Monika

Estrella Negra, Adrian De Leon, Fatin Chowdhury, Justin Chin, Ako Castuera, Emalani Case, and Dionne Brand, whose thoughtfulness and teachings inform these poems

all the unnamed ones who have touched and changed me when our paths have crossed

Asian Arts Freedom School and Lost Lyrics for igniting a communal spark of creativity within me

Canada Council for the Arts, the British Columbia Arts Council, the Writers' Trust of Canada, and Diaspora Dialogues for the financial and professional support which allowed me to complete this collection.

PHOTOGRAPHS

The images interspersed throughout this book, all taken before the onset of WWII, are part of Haru Yamashiro's personal photography collection. I imagine Auntie Haru, my grandmother's older sister, transported these photographs from her pre-war home in California's Imperial Valley to the desert prison barracks of Poston. After the family's release from Poston, I imagine she preserved the photos over the decades first in Chicago and then in Los Angeles' Crenshaw District. For all the photographs, the photographer is unknown.

pg. 13 — *This Afternoon Sky Rises Like a Broken Commodity*

pg. 29 — *The Port of Call is Indefinite, But For The Children We Smile* (Santos, Brazil — 1938)

pg. 47 — *We Keep Talking About Today's Commerce, There Is Still Space For Negotiations Between Us* (My great-grandfather Taro Yamashiro [left] speaks with an unknown man in California's Imperial Valley)

pg. 61 — *We Are Estranged But Our Lives Are Growing Into Recognizable Trees* — (Westmoreland, California, circa 1930)

TEXT

pg. 6 — This poem was written after listening to Bedour Alagraa's lecture "Against the 'Narrative Condemnation of the Earth': The Interminable Catastrophe Breaks." It references diasporic Okinawan scholar Ben Kobashigawa's introduction to Paul Kōchi's *Imin No Aiwa (An Immigrant's Sorrowful Tale)* that states "time has eroded the difference [between Okinawans and other Japanese], which . . . has little meaning in an American context."

pg. 7 — This poem contemplates how those with roots in Okinawa Prefecture experience the event that has come to be known singularly as the Japanese American incarceration.

pg. 9 — The line 'you are never undertaken all at once and never once and for all" references the line "crossings are never undertaken all at once, and never once and for all" from the final chapter of *Pedagogies of Crossing: Meditations on Feminism, Sexual Politics, Memory, and the Sacred* by M. Jacqui Alexander.

pg. 11 — This poem references Wendy Matsumura's *The Limits of Okinawa: Japanese Capitalism, Living Labor and Theorizations of Community.* Matsumura's research highlights how Japanese imperial policy in Okinawa at the turn of the 20th century led to the destruction of the collective ownership of the Yanbaru Rainforest and the banning of Okinawan cultural and spiritual practices. The encroachment of the Japanese state on daily living was the backdrop for my great-grandfather's emigration from Okinawa to Mexico in 1904.

pg. 34 — This poem references my experience at the Worldwide Uchinanchu Festival. According to the festival's website, the gathering, which is organized specifically for the Okinawan diaspora, takes place every five years and is meant to "promote Okinawan soft power both in Japan and abroad, and use [the] island's charms and possibilities to open up a path to the future."

pg. 45 — In Okinawan cosmology, *nirai kinai* refers to the resting place of the gods, a location that is conceptualized as existing either past the horizon or at the ocean's depths.

pg. 55 — This poem references the ongoing construction of a U.S. Military Base at Oura Bay in Henoko in Northern Okinawa. In order to construct the base, parts of the bay, which is home to extensive networks of coral reefs, are being reclaimed using soil from other parts of the island. The oceanic heart of this poem was clarified through a Palo Mayombe divination with diviner Tata Rompe Pecho.

pg. 57 — This poem draws inspiration from a partially redacted report titled "An Anthropological Study of the Significance of the Dugong in Okinawa Culture" prepared for the U.S. Marine Corps. The report investigates the cultural importance of the dugong and interrogates how the construction of a new U.S. military base would affect the people of Okinawa's relationship with the animal. This poem also references the annual Ungami Matsuri, a harvest festival organized by the villagers of Shioya Bay in Ōgimi-Son.

pg. 63 — I am indebted to Akiko Agarie, a reporter with the Ryūkyū Shimpō who published an article about my return to the island after generations of estrangement. Toyo-san, a relative and spiritual leader in Taminato, my ancestral village, recognized a photo of my great-grandparents included in the article, allowing me to reconnect with my great-grandmother's nieces and nephews and visit the village where my great-grandparents grew up.

Adnan, Etel. *Paris, When It's Naked.* The Post-Apollo Press, 1993.

Chu, Huei-chu. "Deauthenticating Indigeneity." *Amerasia Journal*, vol. 41, no. 1, 2015, pp. 37–52.

Sakihara, Mitsugu, et al. *Okinawan-English Wordbook: A Short Lexicon of the Okinawan Language with English Definitions and Japanese Cognates.* University of Hawai'i Press, 2006.

Stewart, Frank, et al. "Two Poems." *Living Spirit: Literature and Resurgence in Okinawa.* University of Hawai'i Press, 2011.

Taira Bintaro. *My Favorite Okinawan Poems.* 1969.

Wynter, Sylvia, and Demetrius Lynn Eudell. *We Must Learn to Sit Down Together and Talk About a Little Culture: Decolonising Essays, 1967-1984.* Peepal Tree Press, 2022.

SHŌ YAMAGUSHIKU is an independent writer and researcher. He writes from the homelands of the Lekwungen and W̱SÁNEĆ peoples (Victoria, B.C.). *shima* is his first poetry collection.